SALVATION

Karyn Henley

STANDARD PUBLISHING

Cincinnati, Ohio

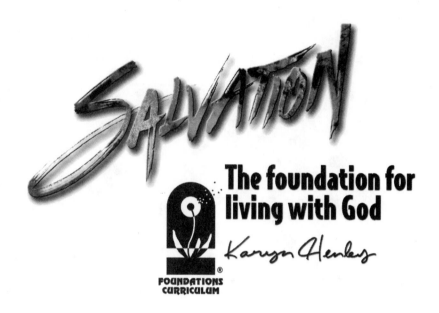

SALVATION

The foundation for living with God

Karyn Henley

FOUNDATIONS CURRICULUM

Published by Standard Publishing, Cincinnati, Ohio
A division of Standex International Corporation

Credits
Cover design by Brian Fowler
Interior design by Jeff Richardson
Cover and inside illustrations by Ed Koehler
Project editors, Jim Eichenberger, Ruth Frederick, Linda Ford

07 06 05 04 03 02 01   5 4 3 2
ISBN 0-7847-1215-8
Printed in the United States of America

TABLE OF CONTENTS

Table of Contents

Introduction 5

Suggested Bible Study Helps 8

1 Saved From What?...9
Colossians 1:13

2 Creation and the Fall....................................18
Isaiah 59:2

3 God's Plan and Covenant 25
2 Timothy 1:9

4 Sacrifices and the Holy of Holies.....................32
John 1:29

5 God So Loved...38
John 3:16

6 Eternal Life...45
John 5:24

7 The Trade...52
Colossians 1:13, 14

8 Forgiven!..58
Isaiah 1:18

9 In Jesus' Name 67
1 Timothy 2:5, 6

10 Jesus "In" Us...73
1 John 4:14, 15

11 The Invitation..78
Romans 10:9

12 Growing Up in Salvation.................................85
2 Corinthians 7:1

13 How to Share the Good News...........................91
Mark 16:15, 16

INTRODUCTION

The Irish poet William Butler Yeats once said, "Education is not the filling of a pail, but the lighting of a fire." In the first temple, the tent of meeting, there was a lampstand. God's instructions were, "Tell the people of Israel to bring you pure olive oil for the lampstand, so it can be kept burning continually. . . . Aaron and his sons will keep the lamps burning in the Lord's presence day and night" (Exodus 27:20, 21, NLT). Today we are God's temple (1 Corinthians 3:16). And our passion, our living love for the Lord, keeps our lampstand burning before him. (See Revelation 2:4, 5.) Our job in the spiritual education of children is to light a fire, a living, growing love for God within them.

The Foundations curriculum can help light that fire. Each of our students is a temple of God. So the goal of the Foundations curriculum is to construct within children the essential foundations upon which they can build (and sustain) a loving, thriving relationship with the Lord. To do this, the Foundations curriculum provides a thorough, step-by-step, in-depth exploration of the following foundations.

Quarter 1: Studying the Bible, The Foundation for Knowing God

Quarter 2: Salvation, The Foundation for Living with God

Quarter 3: Prayer, The Foundation for Growing Closer to God

Quarter 4: Worship, The Foundation for Loving God

This curriculum is intended for use with students in third through fifth grades. Each quarter is independent of the others, so they can be taught in any order. In fact, each quarter can be used as a single unit to fill in a 13-week study at any time of the year and can be followed or preceded by any other curriculum of your choice.

The following arrangement is a suggestion showing how the Foundations Curriculum can be taught in one year. Studying the Bible (September–November), Salvation (December–February), Prayer (March–May), Worship (June–August).

WALK THROUGH A WEEK

SCRIPTURE AND GOAL

The session begins with a Scripture and a simple goal. You may use the Scripture as a memory verse if you wish, or you may use it to support the theme for the day, reading the Scripture when you gather for the first prayer.

INTRODUCTORY ACTIVITY

You can begin your introductory activity as soon as the first student arrives, guiding others to join you as they come into your room. This activity serves two purposes. First, it gives the students something fun to do from the first moment they arrive. Second, it starts thoughts and conversations about the theme of the session. Talking is encouraged. Questions are welcome. Get to know your students. Make it your goal to discover something interesting and special about each one. Let them know that their mission is to discover more about God and about how they can get to know him better every day, so that God becomes their constant companion, their treasured friend, their awesome king.

DISCOVERY RALLY

Gather the students together as a group in preparation for the Discovery Centers.

What's the Good Word? This is a time to read the Scripture for the day. You may also sing a few songs if you want.

Challenge. This is a time to introduce the students to the theme for the day by making challenging statements or asking challenging questions.

Prayer. Choose a student to lead a prayer of blessing for the day's activities, asking God to open your hearts and teach everyone present.

DISCOVERY CENTERS

You will need either one teacher/facilitator for each center, or clearly written instructions that tell the students what they are to do in the center.

The way your class uses Discovery Centers will depend on how much time you have and how many students there are in your class.

- If you have a few students, go together to as many centers as you can in the time you have.
- If you have more than ten students and lots of time, divide into three groups. Send one group to each center and let each group rotate to a different center as they finish the activity, so that each student gets to go to each center during Discovery Center time.

- If you have more than ten students, but little time, divide into groups of three. Number off, one to three in each group. Each student #1 goes to the first center, #2 goes to the second, #3 goes to the third. After each center has completed its activity, the original groups of three come back together again to tell each other what they learned in their centers.
- Or you may choose to let all three centers do the same activity. Choose the one or two activities that you think your students will enjoy most. Divide the students into groups for centers, and once they are there, do not rotate. Instead, let each group do the one or two activities you have chosen.

DEBRIEFING QUESTIONS

If you have time, gather together as a large group at the end of the session to ask and answer questions and discuss the theme and/or other issues on the students' minds.

Review the Scripture for the day.

PRAY

You or a student may close your class time in prayer.

SUGGESTED BIBLE STUDY HELPS

This is by no means a complete list. As you look for these, you will find others that may be just as interesting and helpful.

Bible Handbooks

What the Bible Is All About, Henrietta C. Mears (Gospel Light)

What the Bible Is All About for Young Explorers, Frances Blankenbaker (Gospel Light)

The International Children's Bible Handbook, Lawrence Richards (Word)

The Baker Bible Handbook for Kids, Marek Lugowshi and Carol J. Smith (Baker)

New Unger's Bible Handbook: Student Edition, Merrill Unger (Moody)

Bible Encyclopedias

The Children's Bible Encyclopedia: The Bible Made Simple and Fun, Mark Water (Baker Books)

Bible Dictionaries

International Children's Bible Dictionary, Lynn Waller (Word)

The Baker Bible Dictionary for Kids (Baker)

Bible Fact Books

The Awesome Book of Bible Facts, Sandy Silverthorne (Harvest House)

The Baker Book of Bible People for Kids (Baker)

The Complete Book of Bible Trivia, J. Stephen Lang (Tyndale)

For Teachers and Older Students

Willmington's Bible Handbook, Harold L. Willmington (Tyndale)

Holman Topical Concordance (Holman Bible Publishers)

Holman Bible Dictionary (Holman Bible Publishers)

Children's Ministry Resource Edition (Thomas Nelson)

Manners and Customs in the Bible, Victor H. Matthews (Hendrickson)

Saved From What?

scripture

"God made us free from the power of darkness, and he brought us into the kingdom of his dear son."

Colossians 1:13, ICB

goal

Learn that there are two kingdoms: darkness and light.
Learn that we can be saved from sin and the kingdom of darkness.

INTRODUCTION

Have several flashlights available. Also have plain printer paper and pens, markers, crayons, and/or colored pencils available. As the students arrive, assign each one a partner, or let them choose partners. Tell both partners to get a piece of paper and something to draw with. Tell them to walk around the room, looking for shadows. When they see a shadow they like, they are to place the paper on the edge of the shadow and trace its shape. They may also use flashlights to create shadows on their paper by shining the light onto an object or even onto their hand so that the shadow falls on the paper. They may trace several shadows onto one piece of paper, or they may get a new paper for each shadow they trace. Then they may color the design they have made. If you have time, ask each student to show one or more of his shadow tracings to the group and ask the group to guess what object made the shadow.

DISCOVERY RALLY

Gather the students together in a large group.

WHAT'S THE GOOD WORD?

Choose a student to read the Scripture for the day.

THE CHALLENGE

Hold up a flashlight. Say: **Tell me about an occasion when you had to use a flashlight. Is there such a thing as a "flash-dark"?** Darkness is simply the absence of light. Any time light shines into the darkness, darkness is moved aside. But darkness cannot move light aside. Darkness is here only if light leaves.

Also tell the students some other facts about light:
1) **Light travels at an extremely high speed—186,000 miles per second!**
2) **We are able to see objects when they are illuminated by a light source, because they reflect light back to our eyes.**

Then tell the students that in their Discovery Centers today they will find out about two kingdoms: one called kingdom of darkness and one called kingdom of light.

PRAYER

DISCOVERY CENTERS

1. THE TWO KINGDOMS MURAL

Before the session, roll out about 9 feet of butcher paper along a wall or across the floor. Divide it into three 3-foot sections with a light pencil line between each section. Create overhead transparencies with the art from pages 16 and 17. Project the transparencies on the paper and trace the two castles and landscapes. Place The Kingdom of Light scene on the left side and The Kingdom of Darkness scene on the right.

> **MATERIALS**
> copies of The Kingdom of Light (page 16) and The Kingdom of Darkness (Page 17), overhead transparancies, butcher paper, markers, crayons, glue stick or tape

For the first group of students who come to your center

DO: Divide the students into two groups. The first group works on the far left section of The Two Kingdoms mural. Students should color the castle and landscape to represent the kingdom of light. They should label it "The Kingdom of Light." The second group works on the far right section of the mural. Students should color that castle and landscape to represent the kingdom of darkness. They should label it "The Kingdom of Darkness."

For the second and third groups of students at your center

DO: These students will bring pictures of "traps" from Discovery Center #3. They should take turns gluing these pictures in the center section of the mural. As they glue their pictures on, they should tell you why these things might be traps to sin. If the previous group has not finished coloring their parts of the mural, these students may help finish the castles and landscapes.

Leave the mural on the classroom wall for this quarter. You will need it again in Session 6.

If you have time, let the students look up Scriptures that tell about the two kingdoms. Let them write the Scripture references in the section of the mural that the reference describes. You may use some of the references in the discussion section below as well as Isaiah 65:17-25; Revelation 21:1-8, 23-27; and Luke 16:19-31.

DISCUSS: **Why is God's kingdom called the kingdom of light? Why is the other kingdom called the kingdom of darkness? Who is the ruler of the kingdom of darkness? Which ruler is stronger: God or Satan? What is the king of the kingdom of darkness like?** (See John 8:44; 1 Peter 5:8; John 10:10; Isaiah 14:12, 13; Luke 10:18; Mark 4:15; 2 Corinthians 11:14; Revelation 12:9.) **What is the King of the kingdom of light like?** (See 1 John 4:8; Exodus 34:5-7; 2 Chronicles 6:14; 2 Chronicles 14:11; Deuteronomy 4:7; Isaiah 64:4, 5a; Psalm 25:14; Psalm 23. Choose verses most helpful to your students.)

NOTE: It is important that the students understand that these two kingdoms are the only two choices available to us. People are in one or the other. There is no in-between. Erase the light pencil line that divides the mural into three sections. Draw a line down the center, dividing it into two sections now. People are in the kingdom of darkness automatically unless they have made the *choice* to be saved. None of us is good enough to live forever with the almighty perfect God. We were all doomed to live in the kingdom of darkness forever. That's why God sent Jesus to save us. So when people hear about Jesus, they are able to *choose* to let Jesus save them from the kingdom of darkness and bring them into his kingdom, the kingdom of light.

2. PAPER CHAINS

DO: Bring a real chain (you can find them at hardware stores) and ask the students to try to pull the links apart. Say: **A real chain is strong. What are chains used for?** Draw out the idea that prisoners and slaves were bound by chains. **Why were they bound?**

> **MATERIALS**
> short length of a metal chain, construction paper, scissors, tape

Give each student construction paper and scissors. Have tape available to share. Show the students how to make a ring of paper by cutting a strip of construction paper and curving it around so that the ends overlap. Tape the overlapping ends together. Now show students how to loop another paper strip through the first ring, and make a second ring by overlapping and taping the ends of the second strip. Ask the students to make their own paper chains.

DISCUSS: As the students work on their paper chains, tell them that the Bible says that we are slaves to whatever controls us. Ask different students to read aloud John 8:34, Romans 6:16, and 2 Peter 2:19. Tell the students to write these three verse references onto three different links in their chain. Ask students what being a "slave to sin" might mean.

If students have not been to Discovery Center #1 yet, tell them about the kingdom of darkness and the kingdom of light. Ask: **Does sin come from the kingdom of darkness or the kingdom of light? What did Jesus come to save us from? Why do we need to be saved?**

3. THE TRAP OF SIN

MATERIALS
mouse or rat trap, cheese, old newspapers and magazines, scissors, tape

DO: Bring a mouse trap or a rat trap. Place a small piece of cheese on the trap. Talk about temptation and sin. Say: **Just as the cheese looks good to the mouse, so the things that tempt us look like they will bring us pleasure.** Now set the trap *if you can do so safely.* **Caution:** Make sure that the students keep their fingers away from the trap, and that you keep your fingers out of the way as well. If it's not possible to keep students away, then **don't** set the trap. Ask the students what happens when the mouse falls for the temptation. If you have set the trap, trip it with a long dowel or spoon handle. If you have not set the trap, at least lift up the catch a bit and let it snap down. Compare the trapping of the mouse to what happens when we fall for temptation.

Let students look through old magazines and newspapers, especially the ads, and find pictures of temptations that could trap people into sin. Ask the students to cut these pictures out and take them along to the next group. If this is your last group, gather their pictures and glue them to The Two Kingdoms mural after class.

DISCUSS: As students work, ask them what kinds of temptations students their age have. Talk about the kingdom of darkness and the kingdom of light. Discuss which kingdom temptations come from. Ask a student to read James 1:13-15. Ask: **How can sin trap people? What are some things that might help you say no to temptation?**

DISCOVERER'S DEBRIEFING

If you have time to review, gather as a large group and discuss your young discoverers' findings. Ask the following questions:

- What is the most interesting thing you discovered today?
- What did you learn today that you did not know before?
- Name the two kingdoms that rule the world today. Describe them.
- Are these two kingdoms equal in power? If not, which is stronger and why?
- What do we need to be saved from? Why?
- How could someone become a "slave to sin"?
- How can sin be a trap?

Review the Scripture for today.

Pray, thanking God for his power and his kingdom of light. Thank him for sending Jesus to save us from the kingdom of darkness. Ask God to help us stay away from the trap of sin and the slavery of sin.

ADDITIONAL BIBLE BACKGROUND

Additional Bible Background
le Background

During this lesson, students may ask questions about Satan, or the devil. It is always appropriate to let students ask questions, even if you don't know the answers. Here is some information that may help, if they ask.

The word we use as the name *Satan* means "enemy" or "accuser" in Hebrew. Students may have heard people call Satan "the enemy." It seems that he and the fallen angels have been around since the beginning of the earth. Most scholars believe that Satan was once a perfect being, but that his pride and ambition for power caused his fall (Isaiah 14:12). He tempted Eve in the Garden of Eden (Genesis 3:1), he tempted Jesus (Mark 1:13), and he tries to deceive the whole world (Revelation 12:9). But he is never shown to be equal with God in power, ability, wisdom, or in any other way. Hell is the place that God has prepared for Satan and his demons (Matthew 25:41). First John 3:8 (ICB) tells us that "the devil has been sinning since the beginning" but that Jesus came to "destroy the devil's work."

If students seem to be frightened to think about the reality of the devil, ask them to read the following Scriptures, which assure us that Satan cannot "get" us: John 10:28, 29; 1 John 4:4; Romans 8:31, 35-39; James 2:19; 4:7.

The Kingdom of Light

The Kingdom of Darkness

Creation and the Fall

Scripture

"It is your evil that has separated you from your God. Your sins cause him to turn away from you."

Isaiah 59:2, ICB

Goal

Learn that sin separates us from God.

INTRODUCTION

Set out a stack of plain paper, markers, crayons, rulers, and scissors. As the students arrive, tell each of them that they are to imagine that they have been chosen to design a flag for The Kingdom of Light. Each student may use the material that you've set out to design a flag. When the flags are finished, display them by taping them on or around the castle scene for The Kingdom of Light on the mural that was created last week.

DISCOVERY RALLY

Gather students together in a large group.

WHAT'S THE GOOD WORD?

Choose a student to read the Scripture for today.

THE CHALLENGE

Bring a mirror. Ask a student to look into the mirror and tell you what he sees. The student sees a reflection of himself. Tell students: **God's plan is for other people to see a reflection of God when they look at us. We were created to bring glory to God.** *Glory* **is the revealing of who God is: majestic, powerful, and loving. When we reflect God, we are revealing or showing by our lives how wonderful, loving, and powerful God is. That is what we mean when we say that we "glorify" God or "bring him glory." That is one reason sin is so bad. It does not reflect God. It does not show who he is or bring him glory.** Ask students if lying shows how wonderful and loving God is. Ask students if complaining shows how wonderful and loving God is. Ask them to think about the Scripture for today. Sin separates us from God. Tell students that they will learn more about this in their Discovery Centers today.

PRAYER

DISCOVERY CENTERS

1. THE STORY IN A PAPER CUP

DO: Give each student a paper bathroom cup that has a light or plain design on it. Each student should then turn her cup upside down and draw a face on it. Then ask everyone to stand.

> **MATERIALS**
> paper cups

Tell the students to hold their right hands out, palm up. Tell them to place the cup on their palm. Tell the students: **The cup represents Adam. The palm represents**

God. In the beginning Adam and God had a very close relationship. God provided everything that Adam needed. Adam trusted God and obeyed him. They walked together and talked together like good friends.

Ask the students to tell you what happened next. **Yes, Satan tempted Eve (and Adam through Eve) not to trust God. Satan said she could become wise like God. God had said that if Adam and Eve ate the fruit, they would die. Satan said, "You won't die!" Was Satan lying or telling the truth?**

Then ask each student to place the cup on the floor. They should then resume the position they were in before: right hand extended, palm up. Tell students: **Since Adam and Eve disobeyed, they were separated from God. The Bible says, "It is your evil [sin] that has separated you from your God."** (See Isaiah 59:2, ICB.) **Adam and Eve wanted to do things their own way, to be wise enough to provide for themselves instead of trusting God to provide for them. So God allowed them to find out what it was like to have to provide for themselves. Ever since that time, people have been choosing to sin, although many people have tried to find a way to get back into relationship with God.**

Tell the students to try to get the cup to jump back up into their hand. Motion to it to jump up. Tell it, "Jump up." Ask: **Will the cup ever be able to jump back up into your hand?** (No.) **People cannot get back into a right relationship with God, either. That's bad news, not just for people, but also for God, because God wants to have a relationship with us. God loves us. So God did something amazing.**

Ask the students to slowly reach down and touch the cup. Say: **God came to earth in the form of a man. Who? Do you know the name of Jesus that means "God with us"? It's "Emmanuel." God sent his Son to the earth to live as a perfect man, and to die as punishment for our sins.**

Ask students to pick up their cups and replace them in their right palms. **Now all people can be in a right relationship with God and can have eternal life with him.**

The difference between the cup and us is that we have choice. We can choose to say yes to Jesus and let him bring us back into relationship with God, or we can choose to say no. Ask students why a person might say no.

If you have time: Ask each student to repeat the main points of the story using the cup at each point.

2. SEPARATING

MATERIALS

two clear plastic jars with lids, water, vegetable oil, whipping cream, prepared index cards, salt, knife, and crackers (optional), one set of Letter Cards (page 24) for each student, copied and cut apart

DO: Bring two clear plastic jars with lids. Let students pour water into one jar until it is about one-third full. Let them add vegetable oil until the jar is half full. Let a student pour 1/2 cup of whipping cream into the second jar. Put the lids on both jars. Ask students to begin shaking the jars. After one student has shaken a jar, he passes it to the next student. When all the students have had a chance to shake the oil/water jar, let them place it in the center of the group and observe it. Keep the jar of cream going around the group for about 5 minutes, until butter forms. Set this jar in the center of the group.

DISCUSS: Talk about what happened in each jar. **Why did these things separate? What other kinds of things get separated?** (Dirty clothes before they are washed, clutter that is being cleaned up, two people who are fighting, eggs in certain recipes, and so on.)

DO: Give each student a set of your prepared letter cards. Ask the students to separate the letters, first taking out the letters that spell "us." Ask them to unscramble the letters that are left (God).

DISCUSS: **What separates us from God. Why? What are some sins that students your age might commit? Is there something that can bring us back to God? If so, what?**

If you have time: While you are discussing our separation from God, pour the liquid off the butter, stir a pinch of salt into the butter, and serve it to the students on crackers.

3. GOD PROVIDES; WE GLORIFY

Before the session, cover a small paper plate with aluminum foil. Punch a hole in the plate and thread a ribbon or yarn through the hole so that it will fit around a student's neck and hang down like a medal.

MATERIALS
small paper plates, aluminum foil, ribbon or yarn, markers, several flashlights

DO: Choose one student to stand in front of the others. Distribute the flashlights to several other students. Tell the group to imagine that this student has run a race in the Olympics and has won the gold medal. Place the medallion around this student's neck. Ask the students with flashlights to shine them like spotlights on this student.

DISCUSS: Tell the students that this Olympic winner is receiving the glory when he stands in the spotlight. He is being shown for who he is and what he has done. Ask: **What other people receive glory for who they are and what they've done?** (Famous athletes, movie stars, government leaders.) **These people are talked about; they are "in the spotlight." They are shown for who they are and what they've done.**

DO: Give each student a small paper plate. Let each student cover a plate with foil and make a medallion. Ask them to write on the medallion with a permanent fine-tipped marker "God provides; we glorify."

DISCUSS: How do we give glory to God? We sing about him and praise him. But we usually don't think of another very simple way to glorify God: trusting him, allowing him to provide for us. When we trust God and allow him to provide for us, we are showing other people who God is and what he has done. We are showing people God's true nature of love.

In the beginning, God provided everything Adam and Eve needed. But Adam and Eve chose not to trust God or rely on him to provide for them. They chose to rely on themselves to provide their own wisdom. They ate the fruit to become wise like God. Ask the students why that was a sin.

Sin separates us from God. How can we now get back into a good relationship with God? Can we save ourselves? We trust God to save us. How does he do this?

When we are back in true relationship with God, he provides for us. That's because he is the heavenly Father and we are his children. When we trust him and allow him to provide for us, he gets the glory. So God provides. We glorify.

DISCOVERERS' DEBRIEFING

If you have time to review, gather as a large group and discuss your young discoverers' findings. Ask the following questions:
- What is the most interesting thing you discovered today?
- What did you learn today that you did not know before?
- What separates people from God? Why?
- How can people get back into relationship with God?
- What does it mean to get glory?
- How do we give God glory? Why is it important to glorify God?
- When we have been saved and are in a Father/child relationship with God, what is God's job? (God's job is to provide for us.) **To provide what?** (God provides everything we need for life and godliness. See 2 Peter 1:3.) **What is our job?** (Our job is to glorify God. See Psalm 50:15, NLT.)

Review the Scripture for today.

Pray, thanking God for providing a way for us to be his children so that sin no longer separates us from him.

Letter Cards

Before class, make enough copies of this page so that you will have one copy for each student. Cut apart the cards, making sure that each set is complete. You may wish to put each set of cards in separate envelopes.

God's Plan and Covenant

Scripture

"It is God who saved us and chose us to live a holy life. He did this not because we deserved it, but because that was his plan long before the world began—to show his love and kindness to us through Christ Jesus."   2 Timothy 1:9, NLT

Goal

Learn that salvation means restored relationship with God. Learn that salvation was God's plan, promise, and blessing from the beginning.

INTRODUCTION

As students arrive, tell them that you want them to make up new handshakes and try them out on each other. The only rule is that the handshake has to be safe. It can't hurt the other person.

DISCOVERY RALLY

Gather students together in a large group.

WHAT'S THE GOOD WORD?

Choose a student to read the Scripture for today.

THE CHALLENGE

Ask students if they have heard the word *religion*. Ask them what kinds of religions they have heard about. Say: **Religions are beliefs about spiritual life. Religions are built around people's ways to find or explain God. Religions try to show people how to live "happily ever after." But people, all by themselves, cannot get out of the kingdom of darkness and into the kingdom of light. Why? Because sins separate us from God, and everyone sins. Even when people try to be perfect, they can't do it. Only God has the plan to bring people into the kingdom of light and into relationship with him.**

Tell students that they will learn more about God's plan and promise in their Discovery Centers today.

PRAYER

DISCOVERY CENTERS

1. COVENANTS

DO: Ask your volunteer to explain what a notary public does and why. Give each student a piece of plain paper and have the notary imprint the seal on each student's paper.

DISCUSS: Tell students that agreements and promises are often called *covenants.* Ask: **Can you think of some kinds of covenants that people might make today?** (Marriage, business contracts, the borrowing of money.) **The notary's seal is a sign**

of that agreement or covenant. What are some other signs of covenants? (Wedding ring, handshake, the sign "cross my heart and hope to die," the rainbow given after the flood.)

Ask: Do any of you have pierced ears? In Bible times, people could keep a Hebrew slave for only six years. Then the slave had to be set free. But if the slave wanted to stay with his master for the rest of his life, he had to have his ear pierced. It was a sign of this agreement or covenant between him and his master. (See Exodus 21:2-6; Deuteronomy 15:12-17.)

DO: Give each student a button and a twist-tie or chenille wire. Show them how to thread the wire or tie through the button holes and around a finger to make a ring. When the ring fits the finger without being too tight, they twist the wire to secure it and cut off the excess length of wire. Now give each student a small piece of modeling clay. They are to flatten this on their papers and then press the ring into the clay to make a seal. In Bible times, kings sealed important documents and "covenants" with their own seal that was on a signet ring.

DISCUSS: As the students work, tell them: **God made a promise, a covenant with Abraham to bless the whole earth through him. God wanted to provide for Abraham's people (called the Israelites, Hebrews, or Jews) so that Abraham's people would bring him glory (remember the previous session). Then the whole world would see how great God is and would come to God. But the Israelites did not keep the covenant. They did not trust and obey God. So God promised a *new* covenant.**

Ask students to read Jeremiah 31:31-34. Ask them what this new covenant is and how God kept this covenant to forgive people. Ask a student to read Luke 22:20. **When God forgives us, that brings us back into relationship with him. He is our Father in heaven and we can be his children.**

2. STAR PROMISES

MATERIALS
copies of the Constellations handouts (pages 30, 31), construction paper, white crayons or star stickers

DO: Give each student a copy of the Constellations handouts, a sheet of black construction paper, and a white crayon or star stickers. Ask them to use the crayons or stickers to copy some of the constellations on their papers.

DISCUSS: As the students work, read Genesis 12:1-3 and Genesis 22:15-18 aloud. **From the very beginning, God had his plan for saving the world. The stars were a sign God used to explain his covenant to Abraham.** Ask the students how many people were going to be blessed through Abraham's family. Ask students what this blessing for all people is.

Being able to live with God forever (God being our Father in heaven and we being his children) is the great blessing for all people. But we can only have a Father/child relationship with God if we don't live in sin (because sin separates us from God). Ask students how we become sinless.

3. MAPS TO EAT

MATERIALS
small paper plate, aluminum foil, globe or world map, refrigerated crescent roll dough, flour, sandwich bags, marker

Before the session, use a small plate to trace a circle onto aluminum foil. Cut out one foil circle for each student.

DO: Ask the students to wash their hands before this activity, or pass around the hand wipes or waterless hand sanitizer. Then give each student a triangle of dough from a container of ready-made refrigerated crescent roll dough. Also provide flour to dust students' hands with if the dough gets too sticky.

Tell the students that the circle of foil will be a map. The foil will represent the water. Ask them to form the dough to make the land on the foil map circle. Tell them to use a globe or map of the world for reference. When they have finished, you may bake the foil circles in an oven according to the directions on the package of dough. Or you may let each student place his foil map into a zip-locking sandwich bag. Use a permanent marker to write on the bags the temperature and the time that the rolls are to be cooked. (For example: 350 degrees, 10 minutes.) Then each student can have an adult help bake the map at home.

DISCUSS: As the students work, tell them about God's covenant with Abraham. (For a sample of how to word this, see the two previous activities.)

Ask: How many people did God intend to bless? How did God bless the whole world? God saved us by sending Jesus. This means that we can have a good relationship with God again. He can be our Father and we can be his children. Saving us was God's plan, promise, and blessing from the beginning.

DISCOVERERS' DEBRIEFING

If you have time to review, gather as a large group and discuss your young discoverers' findings. If you have baked the foil maps from Discovery Center #3, you may want to pass these to the students so they can snack as you talk. Ask the following questions:

- What is the most interesting thing you discovered today?
- What did you learn today that you didn't know before?
- What is a covenant?
- What are some signs of covenants today?
- What was God's covenant with Abraham?
- How many people did God intend to bless through Abraham?
- How did God bless all people?
- What was God's new covenant, and who made it?
- What does God want our relationship with him to be? Why?

Review the Scripture for today.

Pray, thanking God for keeping his promises. Thank God for his covenant with Abraham and his new covenant with us through Jesus.

Constellations

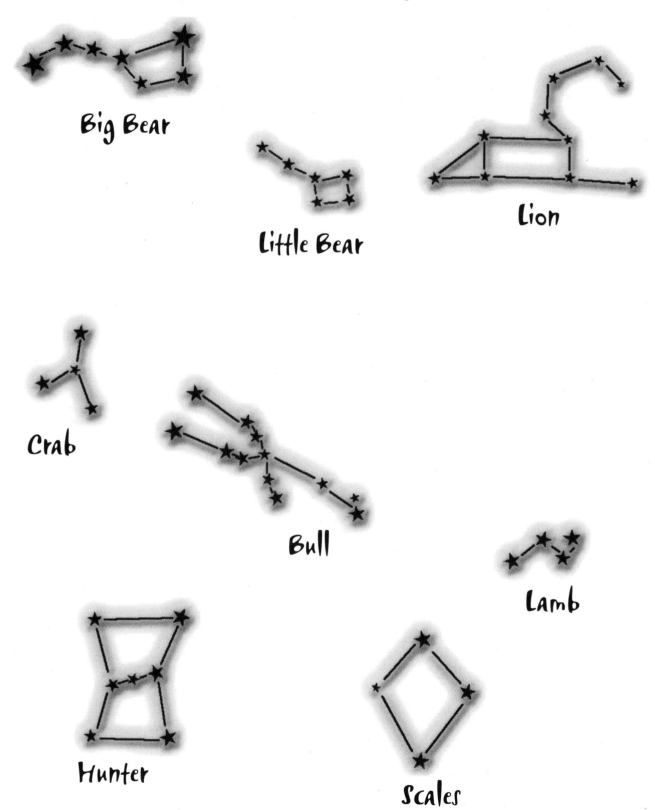

Big Bear

Little Bear

Lion

Crab

Bull

Lamb

Hunter

Scales

Constellations

Eagle

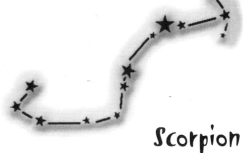

Scorpion

Fish

Swan

Shepherd

Crowned King

Woman on a
Throne

Sacrifices and the Holy of Holies

Scripture

"John saw Jesus coming toward him and said, 'Look, the Lamb of God, who takes away the sin of the world!'"
John 1:29

Goal

Learn some of the ways in which God's people tried to establish a right relationship with God and how Jesus accomplishes this for us.

INTRODUCTION

Ask a Red Cross representative to visit your classroom for the introduction time. Ask this representative to bring some of the stickers they give to those who give blood, or bumper stickers they give as advertisements for the Red Cross. Ask for the stickers that say "Blood is life" if they are available. Try to get at least one sticker for each student. The representative may also bring any other pamphlets that you feel would be useful for your students. As the students arrive, introduce them to the representative and ask this person to tell the students about blood types and why it is important for people to give blood. Let the students ask this representative questions about giving blood.

DISCOVERY RALLY

Gather students together in a large group.

WHAT'S THE GOOD WORD?

Choose a student to read the Scripture for the day.

THE CHALLENGE

Ask: **How many of you play baseball or watch baseball? Do you know what a "sacrifice bunt" is?** It's when a batter purposely taps the ball lightly rather than taking a full swing. Done successfully, a bunt allows a runner to get to the next base at the cost of the batter himself being put out. **Why would a batter make such a sacrifice?** In this case, a batter gives up his chance to get on base for the purpose of making it easier for a player already on base score a run.

A sacrifice is when someone gives up something valuable for the good of someone else. Parents sometimes sacrifice the privilege of buying things they want in order to save money to send their students to camp or to college. As the students learned earlier, some people sacrifice their own blood so that other people can live. Tell students that they will learn about the greatest sacrifice in their Discovery Centers today.

PRAYER

DISCOVERY CENTERS

1. DOORPOSTS

DO: Give each student a paper lunch bag and a large paper plate. You will also need red water-soluble washable paint and small paintbrushes. Ask the students to open the bags and turn them upside down, setting them on the plates. These represent the houses of God's people during the time they were slaves in Egypt. Ask the students what it meant for God's people to be in slavery.

MATERIALS
paper lunch bags, large paper plates,
red water-soluable paint,
small paintbrushes, pencils

Ask the students to tell you about some of the plagues that God sent on the land of Egypt when Pharaoh would not set God's people free. (You can find these in Exodus 7–11.) Ask a student to read Exodus 12:21-23.

Then ask the students to draw a door on each house. While they do this, set out cups of the red paint and the small paintbrushes. Ask the students to paint around the doors of their paper bag houses with the red paint to represent the lamb's blood that God told his people to put on their doorposts.

DISCUSS: What would have happened to a family if they had not painted the blood on their doorposts? Why do you think God chose to have them paint with blood? What does blood represent, and why is it important? As the Red Cross says, "Blood is life." The blood on the family's doorposts showed that the people accepted God and his ways. So they were saved.

Refer to the Scripture for today. John knew about the Passover lamb and the blood on the doorposts. Why would John call Jesus the Lamb of God? What did Jesus sacrifice for us? When we accept Jesus and his blood, what "passes over" us? Remind students of the kingdom of darkness.

2. JUMPING SHEEP

MATERIALS
jump rope

DO: Stretch the rope straight across the floor and place one student at each end. Ask these students to hold the rope taut a few inches above the floor. Ask the students if they've ever heard of "counting sheep" to get to sleep. Tell the students that they are going to do a sheep jump and count how many of them can jump over the rope "fence." The students then take turns jumping over the rope. Count them as they go over. Then ask the two rope holders to raise the rope a few inches. The other students jump over it again, counting "sheep." Continue this until the rope is too high for any sheep to get over.

DISCUSS: Think now about the rope going higher and higher. This represents people sinning more and more. Ezra wrote, "Our sins are higher than our heads and our guilt has reached to the heavens" (Ezra 9:6). Before Jesus came, God's people had a special day once a year when their sins would be taken away. It was called the "Day of Cleansing" or the "Day of Atonement." The high priest, the man in charge of the worship tent or temple, would kill a goat and take the goat's blood into the Most Holy Place (See Leviticus 16.) "Holy" means set apart for God. This was a place where no one could go but the High Priest. The goat was called a "sacrifice." What was sacrificed or given up? Why? What does blood represent? "Blood is life." Sacrificing a goat or lamb or bull showed that God takes sin seriously; sin always hurts someone. The goat had to be sacrificed every year. Why don't we sacrifice goats and lambs and bulls now? Why is Jesus called the Lamb of God?

3. THE MOST HOLY PLACE

MATERIALS
plain, unbleached muslin cut into 12-inch squares; blue, purple, and red fabric markers or paint; scissors, paper clips, string

DO: Give each student a 12-inch square of plain, un-bleached muslin. Provide blue, purple, and red fabric markers or paints. Ask a student to read Exodus 26:30-33. Tell the students that each square of cloth represents the curtain hanging between the Holy Place and the Most Holy Place. Ask the students to decide which side is the top of the curtain. Then they should use scissors and carefully cut a small hole in each of the top two corners. They are to loop a paper clip through each hole so the curtain can hang. Then they should decorate their curtains with the fabric markers or paints. Hang a string across one wall. As they finish their curtains, the students can hang them on the string using the paper clips as hangers. Keep these curtains in your classroom to use again in Session 9.

DISCUSS: Read Hebrews 9:1-7 aloud to the students as they work. Ask: **Who could go behind the curtain? Why do you think only the high priest could go behind the curtain into the Most Holy Place? Why did he have to bring an offering with him? What was the offering? Why was blood considered so important? Remember the Red Cross slogan: Blood is life.** You can read Leviticus 17:11, "For the life of a creature is in the blood, and I have given it to you to make atonement for yourselves; . . . it is the blood that makes atonement for one's life." *Atonement* means making peace again. **Why don't we have to offer blood today? Why is Jesus called the Lamb of God?**

DISCOVERERS' DEBRIEFING

If you have time, gather as a large group and discuss your young discoverer's findings. Ask the following questions:

- What is the most interesting thing you discovered today?
- What did you learn today that you didn't know before?
- What is a sacrifice?
- Why is blood important?
- What was the Most Holy Place?
- Who could go into the Most Holy Place? How often?
- Why is Jesus called the Lamb of God?

Review the Scripture for today.

Pray, thanking God for Jesus who died, giving his blood so that we could be in a peaceful relationship with God.

ADDITIONAL BIBLE BACKGROUND

Additional Bible Background
le Background

The use of animal blood to make peace with God is in many ways a mystery, even to adults. It's all right to admit this to students. As you try to explain it in part, it may help to think of it this way: sin is serious. It separates us from God. What would you give to be at peace with God? If being in a peaceful relationship with God is the most important thing to you, you'd give up, or sacrifice, the most important thing you had in order to be at peace with him.

What's the most important thing you have? Your own life. But God did not require his people to go that far. Instead he asked them to give the life of something else. That something else was a very important possession to people of that time: a perfect lamb or goat or bull. It showed God that people were willing to give up this animal in exchange for a peaceful relationship with God. The blood took away the barrier of sin that kept people separated from God.

God So Loved

Scripture

"For God so loved the world that he gave his one and only Son, that whoever believes in him shall not perish but have eternal life."   John 3:16

Goal

Learn that God sent Jesus not to condemn us but to save us. Learn that our sins separated Jesus from God at the cross where Jesus paid the penalty for our sins.

INTRODUCTION

Provide some simple board games and/or card games for the students to play (Sorry!, Monopoly, Old Maid, and so on). Games you choose should include penalty cards to prepare students for the discussion in The Challenge section.

DISCOVERY RALLY

Gather students together in a large group.

WHAT'S THE GOOD WORD?

Choose a student to read the Scripture for today.

THE CHALLENGE

Refer to the games the students were playing. Ask: **What is a penalty card? Did your game have penalty cards? If so, what was the penalty for drawing that card?** Ask the students who watch or play football to raise their hands. Then ask those who watch or play baseball to raise their hands. Do the same with soccer, basketball, and so on. Ask: **What kinds of penalties are in those games? There are penalties for doing wrong things in these games, whether we intend to do the wrong things or not. In our lives when we do wrong, we call it sin. There are penalties for sin whether we intend to sin or not.** Tell the students that they will learn about penalties in their Discovery Centers today.

PRAYER

DISCOVERY CENTERS

1. SCRIPTURE IN SIGN LANGUAGE

Before the session, use the John 3:16 Signs handouts to learn how to say John 3:16 in sign language. Practice so that you can show the students how to sign this verse. If you don't have time to practice, make one copy of the handouts for each student.

MATERIALS
copies of the John 3:16 Signs handouts (pages 43, 44)

DO: Teach the students how to sign John 3:16. If you've not yet learned the signs, give each student a copy of the handouts. You can all learn it together.

DISCUSS: Ask a student to read Romans 6:23. **What does this verse mean?** Ask a student to read Ezekiel 18:20. **What does this verse mean? It sounds as if death is**

the penalty for sin. Remind the students about last session's center in which they discussed sacrifices. God did not require the people's lives, but allowed them to sacrifice a lamb or goat or bull as the penalty for sin (Leviticus 5:5, 6). **Is death still the penalty for sin today? Who paid the penalty for us? How? God loved us so much, he died for us, so that we can be in a right relationship with him.**

2. "DEFAULT"

DO: Divide the students into pairs and ask them to arm wrestle or thumb wrestle. They can do this a pair at a time while the others watch, or all pairs can wrestle at the same time.

DISCUSS: Ask the students to think about teams in soccer, football, basketball, baseball, or another sport. Ask: **What would happen if you were on a sports team and the whole team was at the field (or gym) ready to play, but the other team never showed up? Who wins? Sometimes we say that the team who showed up won "by default." That means the winning team didn't really play the game, but they won because the other team didn't show up.**

Compare this now to entering the kingdom of light. Ask a student to read John 3:16-18. Tell students: **Some people think God is watching for people to do wrong so he can condemn them.** *Condemn* means to make them pay the penalty. **But it's really just the opposite. God sent Jesus to save us all, because we were condemned already by our own sins. In other words, the world was already condemned in the kingdom of darkness, but God sent Jesus to bring us into the kingdom of light. However, people have to choose to come into the kingdom of light by believing in Jesus. If they don't, they stay in the kingdom of darkness by default.**

3. FINGERPRINT CROSSES

MATERIALS

paper towels, disposable aluminum pie pan, water-soluble paint, paper, pre-moistened hand wipes

DO: Place several layers of paper towels into a disposable aluminum pie pan. Spread water-soluble, washable paint onto the paper towels. Give each student a piece of plain paper. Ask each student to gently press an index finger onto the paint and then vertically onto the center of his paper. Then ask him to press the same finger into the paint again and then press it horizontally across the vertical fingerprint on the paper. This forms a cross. Ask the students to wash their hands, or provide pre-moistened hand wipes for them.

Then ask the students to listen as you read the last seven things Jesus said before he died. (Verses are quoted from the NIV.)

"Father, forgive them, for they do not know what they are doing." Luke 23:34

To a criminal crucified beside him: "Today you will be with me in paradise." Luke 23:43

To his mother Mary: "Dear woman, here is your son [John]."
To John: "Here is your mother." John 19:26, 27

"I am thirsty." John 19:28

"My God, my God, why have you forsaken me?" Matthew 27:46

"Father, into your hands I commit my spirit." Luke 23:46

"It is finished." John 19:30

Give each student a pen or pencil and ask the students to write, "My God, my God, why have you forsaken me?" below their fingerprint crosses.

DISCUSS: What does the word *forsaken* mean? Why do you think Jesus said, "My God, my God, why have you forsaken me?" Remind them that sin separates us from God (Isaiah 59:2). **Jesus took the blame for our sins. When he died on the**

cross, he carried our sins in himself (1 Peter 2:24). **So at the cross, our sins separated Jesus from God the Father. Jesus' death was the punishment for our sins. He paid the penalty for our sins, dying so that we "shall not perish but have eternal life" (John 3:16).**

If you have time, the students can write some of the other statements of Jesus around their fingerprint crosses.

DISCOVERERS' DEBRIEFING

If you have time to review, gather as a large group and discuss your young discoverers' findings. Ask the following questions:

- What is the most interesting thing you discovered today?
- What did you learn today that you did not know before?
- What is a penalty? What is the penalty for sin?
- Who paid the penalty for our sin?
- Did God send Jesus into the world to condemn people? Explain.
- When Jesus was on the cross, why did he say, "My God, my God, why have you forsaken me?"

Sign John 3:16 as you say it together.

Pray, thanking God for sending his Son, Jesus, to pay the penalty for our sins.

John 3:16 Signs

God

Loved

people

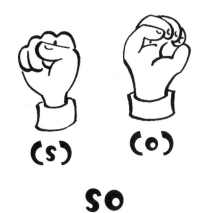

(s) **(o)**

so

John 3:16 Signs

much,

God

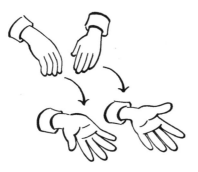

gave

his

son

Eternal Life

Scripture

"Whoever hears my word and believes him who sent me has eternal life and will not be condemned; he has crossed over from death to life."   John 5:24

Goal

Learn that God's kingdom is everlasting. Learn that eternity starts now and never ends.

INTRODUCTION

As students arrive, give each one a copy of the Paper Ring Pattern (page 51). Tell them that today they are going to learn how to walk through a piece of paper. Have scissors available. Ask the students to fold their papers in half on the dotted line and then cut through both halves along the solid lines only. After they have cut where shown, they should shake out the paper gently so that it falls open. Then they can step carefully through the center of the strip and pull it up over them, or they can bring it over their heads down to their feet and step out of it.

DISCOVERY RALLY

Gather students together in a large group.

WHAT'S THE GOOD WORD?

Choose a student to read the Scripture for today.

THE CHALLENGE

Hold up one of the paper rings the students have just made and stepped through. Ask: **Is there a beginning to this ring? Is there an end to the ring?** Show students a ring for a finger. Ask again if there is a beginning or an end? Now ask students to think of time. **Was there a beginning of time? When was it?** (At the creation of the earth.) **Will there be an end of time? Time ends for each person when the person dies. But time for the earth will also end. However, eternity never ends.** Ask a student to read Revelation 21:1-4 and 22:3-5. Tell the students that they will learn about eternal life in their Discovery Centers today.

PRAYER

DISCOVERY CENTERS

1. HEAVEN AND HELL

DO: Hang two paper strips on a wall. Gather your group in front of these two strips. Choose two students to be the secretaries or recorders for your group.

Ask one secretary to write "Heaven" at the top of one strip. Ask the other secretary to write "Hell" at the top of the other strip. Now ask the other students to take turns reading Scriptures about heaven and hell. After each reading, ask the students to give descriptive words for the secretaries to write on the appropriate tape. You may use any or all of the following Scriptures.

Heaven

Deuteronomy 26:15; It is holy (set apart for God).

Isaiah 66:1; God's throne is there.

Matthew 18:10; The angels are there.

Matthew 28:18; Jesus is in charge.

Acts 7:56; Jesus is there at God's right hand.

2 Corinthians 5:1; It lasts forever.

Revelation 21:1-4; There is no death, crying, or pain there.

Revelation 21:22-25; There will be no night there.

Revelation 21:26, 27; Nothing impure or sinful will be there.

Revelation 22:3-5; It lasts forever.

Hell

Matthew 13:42; There will be crying.

Matthew 25:41; It is a place of eternal fire for the devil and his angels.

Matthew 25:46; It will be punishment that lasts forever.

2 Thessalonians 1:9; It is a place of destruction. It is a place away from God.

2 Peter 2:4; There are gloomy dungeons.

Revelation 20:15; There is a lake of fire.

Revelation 21:8; Wicked people will go there.

Both

Luke 16:19-26; Unbelievers suffer in hell while believers are comfortable in heaven. People cannot cross from heaven to hell or from hell to heaven.

DISCUSS: When does eternal life start? It starts when you believe in Jesus. It starts now and goes on forever. God places a special joy and peace in believers' hearts that grows greater and stronger every day, even in times of trouble. (See Galatians 5:22, 23; Philippians 4:4-7.) We get a taste of heaven now, and it grows as we grow in Jesus. Then someday we will experience all of heaven in the way it's described in the Bible. But eternal death starts now as well. Unbelievers don't have the lasting joy or peace that believers have. They taste hell on earth. The emptiness and darkness grows stronger in their lives, and in the end they will experience hell in the way it's described in the Bible. God doesn't put people there; they are already headed there. God sent Jesus to save people from this kingdom of darkness. (See John 3:16, 17.)

2. EARTHLY BODIES, HEAVENLY BODIES

MATERIALS
plastic spoon, plastic disposable picnic plate, and a sponge for each student; grass seed or bird seed; permanent markers, scissors, apple, sharp knife

DO: Tell students to cut off the corners of the sponge to make an oval shape. This will represent a person's head. Ask the students to use the permanent marker to draw eyes about halfway down from the top of the oval. Then they can draw a nose and mouth on the lower half of the sponge. Then they should place the sponge on the plate and very gently spoon water over the area of the sponge above the eyes. Sprinkle the seed onto this area. Tell the students to take this home, keep the seed moist, and watch for "hair" to grow on their sponge person.

DISCUSS: Ask the students to look at the seeds very carefully. Ask them to describe the seeds. Ask them to describe the grass that will grow from the seeds. **Will the grass look anything like the seed? Do flowers look like the seeds they come from?** Cut open an apple and look at the seeds inside. **Does the apple look like the seed?** Then read 1 Corinthians 15:35-58 which compares our earthly bodies with the heavenly bodies we will one day have. (The *International Children's Bible* or *God's Story*, Tyndale, page 690, express this passage well for students.) Read 1 John 3:2. **Does this mean we will be able to move through locked doors like Jesus did in his resurrected body?** (See John 20:19, 26.) Feel free to wonder with students about the possibilities.

3. THE TWO KINGDOMS

MATERIALS
paper and pens, crayons, or markers

DO: Give each student a piece of paper and pens, crayons, or markers. Refer to "The Two Kingdoms" mural created in Session 1. Ask the students to draw the two kingdoms on their own papers. They may draw them to look different than the mural if they want. Ask them to write the Scripture for today at the top or the bottom of their pictures. "Whoever hears my word and believes him who sent me has eternal life and will not be condemned; he has crossed over from death to life" (John 5:24).

DISCUSS: Ask a student to read about the King of the kingdom of light in Isaiah

9:6, 7. Say: **Isaiah says there will be no end to the King's government and his peace. It also says God will reign forever. This kingdom is eternal. Eternity starts now and never ends.** Remind the students that you have been referring to these two kingdoms as the kingdom of light and the kingdom of darkness. But the kingdom of light is sometimes called the kingdom of heaven.

Ask a student to read Matthew 8:11. Ask: **What does this tell us about the kingdom of heaven?** (There is a feast there. Abraham, Isaac, and Jacob are there.) **What else do you know about heaven?**

NOTE: If students have the traditional view of heaven as people sitting on clouds and playing harps, remind them that Revelation 22:3 says that God's servants will serve him. Ask them what they think we might do to serve God in heaven. You can also read Isaiah 11:6-9 and Isaiah 65:17-25. Feel free to admit that you don't understand it all. At the same time, join the students in wondering and thinking about God and his kingdom.

DISCOVERERS' DEBRIEFING

If you have time to review, gather as a large group and discuss your young discoverers' findings. Ask the following questions:
- What is the most interesting thing you discovered today?
- What did you learn today that you did not know before?
- Describe heaven.
- Describe hell.
- Is there any other choice?
- What is eternity?

Review the Scripture for today.

Pray, thanking God for making a way for us to live with him eternally.

NOTE: Before you send the students home, make sure each has a copy of the reproducible note to parents from page 50. It is essential that this note go home in preparation for next week's session.

Dear Parent,

As you may know, we are in the middle of a series of lessons concerning salvation. It is our goal to help each student understand what salvation is, how it is accomplished, and why we need it.

A word that is often used but not easily understood in regard to salvation is the word *redemption*. The truth that God loved us so much that he was willing to buy us back at a high price is an important concept, however.

We are planning what we hope to be a memorable object lesson to help define redemption next week. For that we need your help. We are asking that each student bring two small toys or keepsakes from home. One item is one that the student is willing to give away. The other is one that he or she desires to keep. Please make sure that your child knows which item is which. The "keepers" will be returned, while the "give-aways" will go home with another student.

It is a pleasure to be able to teach your child about this important truth. Thank you for helping us accomplish that task. Feel free to call with any questions.

Teacher _____

Phone _____

Paper Ring
Pattern

1. Fold on the dotted line.
2. Cut this rectangle out. Throw it away.
3. Cut on the other solid lines.
4. Open the paper. Gently shake it out.

The Trade

Scripture

"For he [God the Father] has rescued us from the dominion of darkness and brought us into the kingdom of the Son he loves, in whom we have redemption, the forgiveness of sins."

Colossians 1:13, 14

Goal

Learn that redemption means to buy something back or to free someone from debt or blame. Learn that Jesus took the blame for our sins, and gave us his sinlessness as our own.

INTRODUCTION

Set aside two places in the room for the items that students bring from home: one place for students to put the item they want to keep ("keepers"), and another place to put the item they want to give away ("give-aways"). As students arrive, ask them to put their items in the appropriate places. Then give each student a round disposable foam picnic plate. Each student should cover the plate with aluminum foil so that the foil over the bottom of the plate is very smooth. The foil-covered plate represents a coin. Each student should gently draw on the bottom of the plate with a dull pencil, creating a design for the coin.

NOTE: While the students are designing their coins, take their "keeper" items and line them up along a table at Discovery Center #1. Place the chairs along only one side of the table.

DISCOVERY RALLY

Gather students together in a large group.

WHAT'S THE GOOD WORD?

Choose a student to read the Scripture for today.

THE CHALLENGE

Show the coin designs to the group. Ask: **Have you ever been to a pawn shop?** If they have, ask them to tell about pawn shops. If they haven't, you can describe a pawn shop. **Where does a pawn shop get the items it sells?** Discuss their ideas. **Think of your favorite possession. Imagine that your family needed money, so you sold that possession to the pawn shop. But you loved that possession so much, you worked very hard to earn the money to buy it back. At last you were finally able to buy it back. We would say that you redeemed your favorite possession. We call this redemption.** Tell the students that they will learn more about redemption in their Discovery Centers today.

PRAYER

DISCOVERY CENTERS

1. THE REDEMPTION CENTER

MATERIALS
small items for students to trade and to keep in case they have forgotten to bring their two items from home

DO: Divide your students into two groups: Group A and Group B. Tell the students in Group B to sit at the table. Now distribute the keeper items on the table among the students in Group B. These students set the keepers in front of them as if they are selling them. Tell Group A to retrieve their give-aways from the place where you collected these items. Then *without speaking*, the students in Group A must trade their give-away item for their keeper which is in the possession of a student in Group B. In other words, they are "redeeming" their keepers. (Because the keepers are distributed at random among Group B, it's likely that some Group B members may have more than one item from Group A members. Other Group B members may have none of Group A's items. If this happens, the Group B students who received more than one give-away must share the give-aways with students in Group B who received none.)

Then Group A and Group B trade places. Group B must use the give-aways they brought from home to redeem their keepers from Group A. When the trading is done, each student should have the original keeper he brought from home as well as a new item with which another student redeemed his own keeper. Each student may take home his keeper and his new item.

DISCUSS:
Remind the students that all of us were created by God. **We belong to him. But we all sin. What does sin do? It separates us from God. So we are in the kingdom of darkness because of our sins. But God wants us back, just like you wanted your "keeper" item back. God wants to save us, just like you wanted to save your "keeper." How did you buy your "keeper" back? You traded something else for it. Your "give-away" took the place of your "keeper." How did God buy us back? He traded Jesus for us. Jesus was the "give-away." We were the "keepers." Jesus took our place. He took the blame for our sins and was punished for our sins. His death bought us, "redeemed" us, so we can live in God's Kingdom forever.**

2. SHOE SEARCH

DO:
Ask the students to sit in a circle on the floor. Then they should remove their shoes and place them in front of them. When you say, "Go!" they should pick up their shoes and begin passing them around the circle to the left as quickly as they can. When you say, "Change!" they should quickly pass the shoes to the right. When you say, "Find!" they should try to hold onto their shoes as their shoes get to them in passing. If they accidentally pass their shoes on, the shoes have to go all the

MATERIALS
none needed

way around the circle again. Keep the shoes moving around the circle until they all have their own shoes again.

DISCUSS: Ask the students to briefly tell you the story of Ruth. Then read or ask a student to read Ruth 3:1–4:13. Use a version of the Bible in which the word *redeemer* is used. (The NIV is one of these.) Ask: **What was the relative Boaz going to redeem? In other words, what was he going to buy back? Who actually redeemed the property and got to marry Ruth? How did they make the deal official? When we say that Jesus is our Redeemer, what do we mean? What did Jesus buy back? How? Why?**

If you have time, you may want to play the Shoe Search game again.

3. THE STORY IN YOUR HAND

MATERIALS
copy of The Story in Your Hand (page 57), thread, paper clip, scissors, magnet

DO: For the first part of this activity, learn The Story in Your Hand (page 57). For the second part, tie 15 inches of thread to the end of a paper clip. (You will need one of these for each group of students.) Practice this part of the activity before doing it in class.

Teach the students The Story in Your Hand. This is a way of telling the story of our redemption. Ask the students to repeat the first sign after you, saying the words. Then ask them to repeat the second. Before you learn the third sign, ask them to repeat the first and second together. Then learn the third. Repeat the first, second, and third. Then learn the fourth, and so on.

After the students have learned these hand motions, show them an object lesson with the magnet and the paper clip with thread tied to it. Place the magnet on the table, and place the paper clip far enough away so that it's not pulled toward the magnet. Lay the thread that's attached to the clip on the table so that the thread stretches away from the magnet. Now ask a student to place her hand on top of the thread firmly so that the paper clip is not able to move toward the magnet, even if the magnet attracts the clip.

Explain that the paper clip represents us. The magnet represents God. The thread represents our sin that keeps us away from God. Now slowly move the magnet across the table toward the paper clip until the paper clip is pulled toward the magnet but does not touch it. The thread holds it back.

DISCUSS: How can we set the paper clip free to be drawn to the magnet? (We'll have to cut the string.) **How can we get free to live with God forever?** (We have to get rid of sin.) **How can we cut the string?** (We'll have to use scissors.) **How can we get rid of sin?** (Jesus took the blame and the punishment for our sins. We can be sinless, because Jesus redeemed us. He bought us back.)

Ask a student to snip the thread. Watch the paper clip jump to the magnet. **When we receive what Jesus did for us, God declares that we are sinless and we move into a loving relationship with God.**

If you have time, review the hand signs that tell the story of redemption.

DISCOVERERS' DEBRIEFING

If you have time to review, gather as a large group and discuss your young discoverers' findings. Ask the following questions:

- What is the most interesting thing you discovered today?
- What did you learn today that you did not know before?
- What does *redeem* or *redemption* mean?
- Why do we sometimes call Jesus our Redeemer?
- Why do we need to be redeemed?
- Tell the redemption story with hand motions.

Review the Scripture for today.

Pray, thanking God for redeeming us from sin by sending Jesus to take the blame for our sins and to be punished in our place.

THE STORY IN YOUR HAND

God is perfect. (Point up to God.)

I am not. (Point to self.)

But Jesus came to take the blame. (Form a J.)

He died on the cross, punished for my sins. 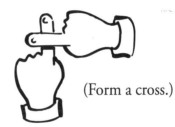 (Form a cross.)

Now I can be perfect.  (Put hands out, palms up.)

All I have to do is ask. 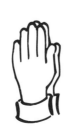 (Form praying hands.)

Forgiven!

Scripture

"Though your sins are like scarlet, they shall be as white as snow." Isaiah 1:18

Goal

Learn that God forgives even the worst sin because Jesus took the blame for our sins and was punished in our place.

INTRODUCTION

As students arrive, give each one a pencil and a copy of the Change-the-Word Game handout (page 66). Tell the students to follow the directions to discover some important words that will help them figure out the Scripture for today.

DISCOVERY RALLY

Gather students together in a large group.

THE GOOD WORD and THE CHALLENGE

Go through the clues of the Change-the-Word Game the students just played and let them give you the answers. Then ask the students to tell you what the Scripture is for today. (They will have discovered it as they finished the word game.) Help students understand that this Scripture shows us how completely God forgives us. Tell the students that they will learn more about God's forgiveness in their Discovery Centers today.

PRAYER

DISCOVERY CENTERS

1. THE STRING STORY

Before the session, tie the ends of each piece of string or yarn together, making a circle. Using The String Story instructions from pages 64 and 65, practice the story yourself.

MATERIALS
copy of The String Story (page 64, 65), 56-inch length of string or yarn for each student

DO. Give each student a circle of string. Divide the class into pairs. Call one person A; the other person B. Show person A how to play the string game with person B as the helper (whose hand gets trapped and freed). Let them practice this a few times. Then they trade. Person B practices the string game while person A becomes the helper whose hand gets trapped and freed.

DISCUSS: Remind the students of Session 1 (in which you demonstrated the trap of sin by using a mouse trap). **How can sin trap us? How can we get free from the trap of sin?** (God sent Jesus to come and free us. His death was the punishment for all sin, for all people. Now we no longer have to live in sin or face the consequences of sin: separation from God both now and forever. God freely forgives us, because Jesus took the blame for our sins.) **What can we do to let God know that we accept this gift of forgiveness from him?**

If you have time, write the word FORGIVE on a chalkboard, dry erase board, or piece of paper. Ask: **What two words make the word FORGIVE? These words are FOR and GIVE. Now switch the order of those two words: GIVE FOR. What did God GIVE FOR us in order to FORGIVE us?**

2. NAILING OUR SINS TO THE CROSS

Before the session, construct a small wooden cross. If you prefer, you can make a cross out of cardboard gift wrap tubes or even poster board. If you choose this option, bring thumbtacks or paper fasteners (brads) to class instead of a hammer and nails.

MATERIALS

a small cross made by nailing a 2-foot length of 1-by-4-inch wood across a 4-foot length of 2-by-4-inch wood; hammer, small tack nails, paper, pencils

DO: Ask students to list some sins that students their age might commit. Then give each student a small piece of paper and a pencil. Ask each student to write on the paper a sin he has done. The students are not to sign their names. They should fold the paper in half. Assure the students that no one will look at the paper. Now the students should take turns nailing their pieces of paper to the wooden cross. If you made a cardboard or paper cross, place it on a firm surface so the students can tack their papers onto the cross. Otherwise, use paper fasteners (brads).

DISCUSS: Ask a student to read 1 Peter 2:24. In the *International Children's Bible*, it says, "Christ carried our sins in his body on the cross. He did this so that we would stop living for sin and start living for what is right." Say: **If you hear someone say, "Our sins have been nailed to the cross," this is what they mean. Jesus was punished for our sins. Now we are forgiven! When we receive God's forgiveness through Jesus, we leave our sins behind. We are free and forgiven! What do we do if we sin again? Does that mean we're trapped again? God's forgiveness is for all our sins whether they are yesterday's sins, today's, or tomorrow's. As long as we keep following God and believing in Jesus, we live in forgiveness. That's good news!**

If you have time, ask a student to read Psalm 103:8-12. Ask: **How far is east from west? No matter how far east you travel, east is still east of you and west is still west of you. East and west are opposite. They are as far apart as you can get. So, how far has God removed our sins from us?**

3. FORGIVEN

MATERIALS
plain white paper, white crayons,
red watercolor paint, paintbrushes

DO: Give each student a piece of plain white paper and a white crayon. Ask the students to write the word *Forgiven* on their papers with the white crayon, pressing down hard to make the letters thick and waxy. Then ask students to paint over their papers with red watercolor paint. The white letters will resist the paint and the word will show up clearly.

DISCUSS: Talk about the Scripture for today: **What does Isaiah 1:18 mean by "sins are like scarlet"? What does it mean when it says "they shall be as white as snow"? Why do we need to be forgiven? Why does God forgive us? How does God forgive us? God forgives even the worst sin because Jesus died to be punished for all sins, even the worst ones.**

If you have time, pour water into a pie pan or cake pan until it's half full. Then let students sprinkle pepper across the top of the water. Tell them that the pepper represents our sins. As the pepper falls on the pure water, the water becomes impure. As we sin, our lives and our hearts become impure. Now give a student a small bottle of dishwashing liquid. Tell the students that this represents God's forgiveness. Ask the student to drip one drop of the dish liquid onto the water right in the center of the pan. The pepper will immediately race to the sides of the pan, representing our sins being taken away by God.

Discoverers' Debriefing
Discoverers' Debriefing

DISCOVERERS' DEBRIEFING

If you have time to review, gather as a large group and discuss your young discoverers' findings. Ask the following questions:

- What is the most interesting thing you discovered today?
- What did you learn today that you didn't know before?
- Why do we need to be forgiven?
- Why do we sometimes say that Jesus "carried our sins in his body on the cross" (1 Peter 2:24, ICB)?
- How can we get God to forgive us?
- Are some sins so bad that we can't be forgiven of them?

Review the Scripture for today.

Pray, thanking God for forgiving our sins through Jesus' death on the cross.

Additional Bible Background
le Background

ADDITIONAL BIBLE BACKGROUND

Students will probably not mention the "unforgivable sin" (Matthew 12:31), and it's best not to introduce it at this time. But if a student asks, or in case you wonder, here is a simple explanation. Earlier in Matthew 12, the Jewish leaders accused Jesus of doing his works by the power of the devil. The Holy Spirit's work is to point out that Jesus is Lord. People can't believe in Jesus and the Holy Spirit and at the same time attribute the Holy Spirit's work to Satan. Saying that the Holy Spirit is evil and that his works are the works of the devil is unforgivable because the person who believes that the Holy Spirit is evil has rejected God's work. That person is not in a position to accept forgiveness.

The String Story

1. String behind pinkie and thumb, crossing palm.

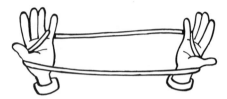

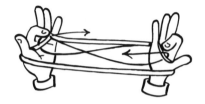

2. Pointer fingers pick up string opposite, from underneath; then pull hands sideways to tighten, revealing a diamond-shaped space in the center.

TEMPTED

3. Partner's hand through diamond from above.

SIN

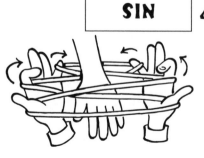

4. Drop string from pinkies and pointers and pull hands sideways to tighten.

TRAPPED IN SIN

5. Pick up string with pinkies.

JESUS CAME

6. Pointer fingers pick up palm string opposite, pull to tighten, forming a diamond space as in step 2.

TO TAKE OUR PUNISHMENT

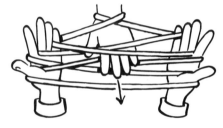

7. Partner's hand up through center diamond.

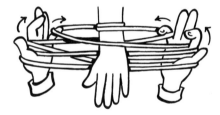

8. Slip string off of pinkies and pointers; pull to tighten . . .

AND NOW

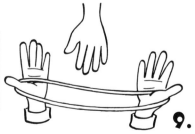

WE ARE FREE!

9. Partner is free.

Change-the-Word Game

Write the answer to the clues in the blanks.

First write a word that means a deep red color:

S ____ ____ ____ ____ ____   Now take two letters out of the word to make

Another word for frighten: S ____ ____ ____ ____

Change one letter of the word to make

Another word for trap: S ____ ____ ____ ____

Change one other letter to make

A sound someone might make while asleep: S ____ ____ ____ ____

Take out one letter and change another to make

A frozen substance that comes down from the sky in cold

weather   S ____ ____ ____

Put the first word in your list above into the first blank.

Put the last word in the last blank.

"Though your sins are like _____,

they shall be as white as _____."   Isaiah 1:18

In Jesus' Name

Scripture

"There is only one way that people can reach God. That way is through Jesus Christ, who is also a man. Jesus gave himself to pay for the sins of all people. Jesus is proof that God wants all people to be saved."   1 Timothy 2:5, 6, ICB

Goal

Learn why we say, "In Jesus' name, amen" at the end of prayers. Learn that Jesus' death allows us to come into God's presence.

INTRODUCTION

Before the session, copy the Jesus stand-up pattern (page 72) to a piece of sturdy cardboard. Cut it out to make a pattern for students to trace. You may wish to make several of these cardboard patterns, depending upon the size of your class.

As students arrive, give each student a large piece of construction paper that has been folded in half lengthwise. Ask students to place the straight edge of the cardboard pattern on the fold. Using a pencil, they should trace the pattern on the paper. Then they can cut through both thicknesses of paper along the traced lines, leaving the letters attached to the baseline at the bottom. Warn students not to cut on the fold. Then fold out the name and stand it up using its "shadow" as the stand.

DISCOVERY RALLY

Gather students together in a large group.

WHAT'S THE GOOD WORD?

Choose a student to read the Scripture for the day.

THE CHALLENGE

Refer to the shadow names that the students made during the introductory activity. Ask: **What do most Christians typically say at the end of a prayer? Why do we say, "in Jesus' name, amen"? Many people say it without even knowing why. It is like a formula or a way of saying, "the end." Is it all right to pray and not end the prayer that way?** Tell the students that in their Discovery Centers today, they will learn why we say, "in Jesus' name, amen."

PRAYER

DISCOVERY CENTERS

1. TEARING THE CURTAIN

DO: Give the students the curtains they made in Session 4. (See Discovery Center #3 in Session 4.) Remind the students that in the worship house (the Old Testament tabernacle and temple, and the New testament temple), there was an area called the Holy Place. Beyond the Holy Place was a special room called the Most Holy Place or the Holy of Holies. Ask: **Do you remember what separated these two rooms?** (A curtain separated them.) **The high priest would enter the**

MATERIALS
curtains made by students in Session 4

Most Holy Place once a year. It was a special place to meet with God and offer a sacrifice for the people's sins.

Ask a student to read Matthew 27:45-54. Ask: **What amazing things happened when Jesus died? What happened to the curtain?** Ask them to think about how tall the curtain was and about how it was torn (v. 51). **If a person had torn the curtain, would that person have torn it from top to bottom or bottom to top? Why? Who tore the curtain?**

Ask the students to tear their curtains from top to bottom. You may need to cut a small slit in the fabric to get the tear started.

DISCUSS: Ask the students why they think the curtain tore. Ask another student to read Hebrews 9:11, 12, 24. **The curtain tore from top to bottom to show that God tore it. The curtain represented separation between people and God. But Jesus made himself to be the sacrifice for our sins, so people are no longer separated from God. The curtain was no longer needed. So when we pray, we can pray directly to God. We don't need a high priest. Jesus is our high priest. So when we come to God in prayer, we come "in Jesus' name."**

If you have time, ask your group to sit in a circle. Number the students. The odd-numbered students hold one piece of their curtain in their left hand and the other piece in their right hand. The odd-numbered students then turn to the student on their right. Everyone together says, "There is only one way to reach God." The odd-numbered students hand the curtain piece from their right hand to the student they are facing. Then everyone says, "Through Jesus Christ, God's Son." Then they hand the curtain piece from their left hand to the student they are facing. Now the even-numbered students have the curtain pieces. They turn to the student on their right and say the same thing. Keep this up until curtains go around the circle and back to their original owners.

2. PASSPORTS

MATERIALS

instant picture camera and film, blue construction paper, silver or gold markers or crayons, real passport

DO: Give each student half of a piece of blue construction paper and provide silver or gold markers or crayons. If you have a real passport, show it to the students. Let them see the pages that contain ink stamps from other countries. Ask the students to fold the construction paper in half and write "Passport" on the front. Take a photo of each student with the instant camera. Let the students glue their photos inside their passport booklets. (If you don't have such a camera available, help the students to make I.D.'s using index cards. Ask them to write their names, height, and hair and eye color on the cards. You may want to furnish a measuring tape to get the measurements.)

DISCUSS: What is the purpose of a passport? What happens if you try to get into a foreign country and don't have a passport? In a way, Jesus is our passport to get to God. Ask a student to read the Scripture for the day, 1 Timothy 2:5, 6. So when we pray to God, we "show" our passport. How do we do this? (We say, "in Jesus' name.") What does "amen" mean? (It means, "yes, let it happen.")

3. VINE AND BRANCHES

MATERIALS

large paper plates, golf-ball sized pieces of modeling clay, lead-free solder wire cut into 1-foot sections, green floral tape cut into 2-foot lengths, scissors, light green paper, red paper

DO: Give each student a plate, a piece of modeling clay, wire, and floral tape. The students should place the clay in the center of the plate. Then they should stick one end of the soft solder wire into it and bend the rest of the wire to make it look like a vine. Ask students to cut out leaves from the green paper and fruit from the red paper. Each leaf or fruit should have a "stem" to help attach it to the vine. Students should wrap their vine in green floral tape. As they wrap the wire, they should pull gently on the tape. This will make it sticky so that it will stay in place. Periodically, the student should place a leaf or fruit next to the vine so that when he wraps the floral tape around the wire, the "stem" of the leaf or fruit is taped to the wire.

DISCUSS: Ask a student to read John 15:5 and then John 14:6. Ask: **Why can't we come to God the Father without going through Jesus?** (Nothing bad or sinful can live in God's presence. We are sinful.) **But Jesus' death was the punishment that paid for our sins. Now we can be sinless. We can talk directly to God and live in his presence. But it's only because Jesus gave his life for us. So when we come to God, we come "in Jesus' name." How did Jesus open the way for us to come to God?**

DISCOVERERS' DEBRIEFING

If you have time to review, gather as a large group and discuss your young discoverers' findings. Ask the following questions:

- What is the most interesting thing you discovered today?
- What did you learn today that you didn't know before?
- What unusual thing happened to the temple curtain when Jesus died?
- What does the torn curtain mean?
- Why do we say, "in Jesus' name, amen" at the end of our prayers?
- Is there any other way to tell God we are praying to him in Jesus' name?
- Is there any other way to reach God other than coming through Jesus?

Review the Scripture for today.

Pray, thanking God for sending Jesus so that we would have a way to come directly to God. Pray "in Jesus' name."

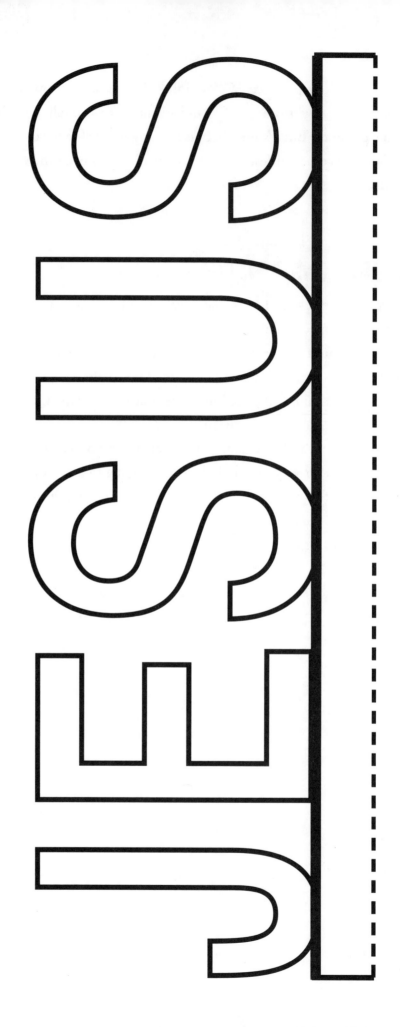

Jesus "In" Us

Scripture

"The Father has sent his Son to be the Savior of the world. If anyone acknowledges that Jesus is the Son of God, God lives in him and he in God."   1 John 4:14, 15

Goal

Learn that when we ask Jesus to be our Lord and Savior, he comes to live within us.

INTRODUCTION

Before the session, obtain at least one used greeting card for every two students. Cut off the front pages of the cards and throw away the back pages. Then turn the front pages facedown and draw a line across the middle to create a top half and bottom half of the card. On the top half write, "Come near to God." On the bottom half write, "and he will come near to you (James 4:8)." Then cut each page along the line that divides it in half. Mix up these half pages.

As students arrive, give each of them one half of a greeting card. They will need to find the person holding the other half. When they match cards, they read the verse on the back. Then they bring the matching halves back to you. When you receive enough halves to shuffle, give students two other random halves, and they can try to find the match for those.

DISCOVERY RALLY

Gather students together in a large group.

WHAT'S THE GOOD WORD?

Choose a student to read the Scripture for the day.

THE CHALLENGE

Ask the students to tell you who loves them. Ask: **Do you know anyone who loves you enough to want to be with you literally *all* the time? God loves us so much he wants to be with us *all* the time. The best way for him to be with us all the time is to come and live right inside us.**

What was the verse on the back of your matched greeting card? How near does God want to be to us? Yes, he wants to live in us. Tell students that they will learn more about Jesus living in us as they go to their Discovery Centers today.

PRAYER

DISCOVERY CENTERS

1. PROFILES

DO: Give each student a large piece of dark colored construction paper and a large piece of manila paper. Divide the students into pairs. Each student should lay his head sideways on the manila paper and have his partner trace around the head to make a profile. (An optional way to do this is to tape the manila paper to a wall, ask the student to stand with his head sideways in front of it, and shine a bright light onto the student. Then his partner can trace around the shadow of his profile.) After the profile has been drawn on the manila paper, the student should cut it out and glue it onto the colored construction paper. Then the student should write JESUS in the head of the profile.

> **MATERIALS**
> large pieces of dark-colored construction paper, large pieces of manila paper, pencils, scissors, glue

DISCUSS: When we ask Jesus to be our Lord (which means "boss" or "king") and Savior, then he comes to live in us. This is a mystery. Ask a student to read Colossians 1:27. Even the apostle Paul said it was a mystery.

Remind the students of the vine they made last week in Discovery Center #3. Ask a student to read John 15:1-4.

What does it mean to have Jesus living in you? Jesus said we would bear "fruit" if we remain in him. What kind of "fruit" grows in us when Jesus lives in us? Read Galatians 5:22-26. When Jesus lives in us, we become more like him. God's Holy Spirit works in us, growing us up to more like Jesus every day.

2. THE ENVELOPE

MATERIALS
index cards, plain envelopes large enough to contain one index card, a variety of markers, stamps, and stickers

DO: Give each student an envelope. Tell each student that the envelope represents her, so the student should decorate the envelope in a way that represents her own personality. Then give each student an index card. Ask each student to write "Jesus" on the card and place it inside the personalized envelope.

DISCUSS: The envelope with the card inside will remind us that if we have asked Jesus to be our Lord and Savior, then he lives within us. Have you ever heard anyone say, "Ask Jesus to come into your heart"? Have you ever asked Jesus into your heart? What does that mean?

Some little children think it means somehow opening up their physical heart and letting Jesus come in. I heard about a small boy who took a bite of sandwich and said, "That bite hit Jesus right on the head!" I also heard about a little girl who asked Jesus into her heart and then said, "His beard doesn't itch!" What were these little children thinking? What does it really mean for Jesus to live inside of you?

3. JESUS IN MY HEART

MATERIALS
blank, unlined index cards;
markers, pens, or pencils

DO: Give each student a card. Tell the students to fold it in half, then open it again. Ask them to draw a heart on the left side of the fold line. Then they should write "Jesus" on the right side of the fold line starting fairly close to the fold. Now ask them to hold the index card at arm's length and focus their eyes on the center fold line. They should then bring the card closer to their eyes very slowly as they continue to look at the fold line. They may need to unfocus their eyes as the card comes closer. At some point, they should see the word *Jesus* jump into the heart.

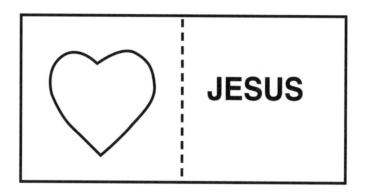

DISCUSS: What does it mean to ask Jesus to come into your heart? The Bible does not tell us to ask Jesus to come into our hearts. What does the Bible say about Jesus living in us? Ask a student to read Roman 8:10. (ICB or NLT versions are easier to understand for this verse.)

Ask another student to read John 17:23, Jesus' prayer to God. What does Jesus say can happen with believers because he lives in them? Ask another student to read 1 John 3:23, 24 and 4:13-16. Then ask the students to discuss what these verses tell them about Jesus living in us.

This is a subject that is difficult even for adults to understand. But it's to be expected that we won't understand everything about God, since he is so much greater than we. God doesn't ask us to understand everything about him. But he does ask that we believe him and trust him.

DISCOVERERS' DEBRIEFING

If you have time to review, gather as a large group and discuss your young discoverers' findings. Ask the following questions:

- What is the most interesting thing you discovered today?
- What did you learn today that you didn't know before?
- Why does God want to live in us?
- When does God come and live within us?
- What do people mean when they say, "Ask Jesus to come into your heart"?
- How do we know that Jesus is living within us?

Review the Scripture for today.

Pray, thanking God for loving us so much that he wants to live within us.

The Invitation

Scripture

"If you use your mouth to say, 'Jesus is Lord,' and if you believe in your heart that God raised Jesus from death, then you will be saved." Romans 10:9, ICB

Goal

Learn that we must all make a choice whether or not to respond to Jesus' invitation to be saved.

INTRODUCTION

Bring small boxes, gift wrapping paper, tape, scissors, bows, gift tags, pens, and index cards. As students arrive, give each one of them a small box and an index card. Ask the students to write "eternal life with God" on the index card. Then they should place the card in the box (folding the card if necessary). They should wrap the box with gift wrapping paper and a bow and then each should write his name in the "To" space on a gift tag. Attach the tag to the box.

DISCOVERY RALLY

Gather students together in a large group.

WHAT'S THE GOOD WORD?

Choose a student to read the Scripture for today.

THE CHALLENGE

Tell the students that there was once a man who was very good actor. He was so good, he was chosen to receive a very special award. Many actors wished they could get this award. But this man was chosen because of his great talent. However, when the time came to present the award, the actor would not take it. He did not want it. He *rejected* it. So he never *received* it. Tell the students that this is a true story. (At the 1972 Academy Awards, Marlon Brando was chosen to receive the Best Actor Oscar for his role in the movie, *The Godfather*. Brando sent a Native American to the stage to refuse the Oscar, protesting the portrayal of Native Americans in Hollywood movies.)

Then choose one of the gifts that was wrapped in the introductory activity. Read the name on the gift tag. Ask the students to imagine that this student's grandmother bought this gift for his birthday. Say: **Inside is something very expensive. His grandmother put this gift on a table and said, "There is a gift on the table for you."** Place the gift on the table. Ask: **Does the student have the gift yet?** (No.) **It's not until the student actually walks across the room, picks it up, and unwraps it that he has it. The gift could sit on the table for a week, or a month, or a year. All that time, it is intended for the grandchild. But the grandchild doesn't have it until the he comes and receives it.**

Tell the students that today in Discovery Centers they will talk about how to receive the greatest gift ever offered to them, if they have not already received it.

PRAYER

what is an invitation?
who sends + gets invitations?
what are invitations used for?
Parties where gifts are usually given?
How many like to get gifts? X-mas-birthday
special occasions.
Read Matt 11:28

DISCOVERY CENTERS

1. THE FEAST

MATERIALS
three small cakes decorated as for a wedding, punch, paper plates, plastic forks, party decorations, party invitations

Before the session, address one party invitation to each student. The party invitation should state the time and place of your session. On one side of the invitation, write "Come to me, all you who are weary and burdened, and I will give you rest" (Matthew 11:28).

after reading Scripture. Ask: what is this leading to. An invitation - a parable -

play game ~~circle~~ gift

DO: Seat the students at a table where you have placed the cake and decorations. Then read Luke 14:15-24. Give each student a party invitation. Ask them to read the Scripture on it, and tell them that this is something Jesus said. Serve the cake and punch.

DISCUSS: As the students eat, talk about Jesus' invitation to come to him. **Why should people come to Jesus? How can people respond to Jesus' invitation?** Ask a student to read Romans 10:9. **First, people have to know that they are sinners and they need to be saved. Why? Yes, the Bible tells us that everyone sins. So people need to admit to Jesus that they have sinned and that they are sorry. They tell Jesus they receive his death as the punishment for their sins. They ask Jesus to save them from sin (or to be their Savior). They tell Jesus they will follow him and let him be in charge of their lives (in other words, they ask him to be their Lord).**

2. THE YOKE

MATERIALS
two pieces of poster board of different colors, scissors

Before the session, make a yoke by cutting out a large circle from the center of each of two different colored pieces of poster board. Each circle should be large enough to allow a student's head to fit comfortably through it with plenty of room to spare. The rest of the poster board or cardboard should hang around the neck and down over the shoulders.

DO: Choose a student to wear a yoke. The student may choose the color of the yoke she wants to wear. Explain that a yoke is a frame made for a person's shoulders in order to carry a heavy load in two equal portions. Tell about oxen and cattle that wore yokes and pulled plows long ago. In some places today where tractors are not used, oxen in yokes still plow the ground. Say: **This yoke represents sin. Sin can make us weary and worried.** Ask a student to read Matthew 11:28-30. Now choose a student to represent Jesus. Place the other yoke on that student. Ask the students what the Scripture said about Jesus' yoke. Then trade the student's yoke for Jesus' yoke. **Jesus took our sins. Now we are forgiven and free.**

DISCUSS: Matthew 11:28-30 is an *invitation* to get free from the yoke of sin. It is also an invitation to have an abundant life. Ask a student to read John 10:10. **What is a full, abundant life? Have you ever gotten an invitation, but didn't go to the event you were invited to? You can say yes or no to an invitation. People can say yes or no to Jesus' invitation. Jesus asks. Each person has the choice of saying yes or no to Jesus' invitation to have sins forgiven.**

3. THE GIFT GAME

Before the session, wrap three gifts, one for each group, with five or six layers of wrapping paper. Inside the gift boxes there should be enough treats (snacks or stickers) for each student in the group.

MATERIALS
three gift boxes, snacks or stickers, gift wrapping paper, audio tape or CD, tape player or CD player

DO: Seat the students in a circle. Turn on the music. While the music plays, the students pass the gift around the circle. When you turn off the music, the student holding the gift unwraps one layer of gift wrapping paper. Turn on the music again. The students pass the gift around again. Continue passing the gift when the music is on, and letting the student holding the gift when the music goes off unwrap one layer. The student who unwraps the last layer chooses another student and calls that student's name. This student must come and receive the gift. Then that student may open the box and share the treats with the group.

DISCUSS: Ask the student who opened the gift: **When your name was called, did you have the gift yet? Could you have said that you didn't want it? What did you have to do to get the gift?** Ask a student to read Romans 6:23. **What is the greatest gift God gave us?** Ask a student to read John 14:1-3. **What does John 14:1-3 tell us about the gift?** Ask a student to read John 14:27. **What does this tell us about the gift?**

DISCOVERERS' DEBRIEFING

If you have time to review, gather as a large group and discuss your young discoverers' findings. Ask the following questions:

- What is the most interesting thing you discovered today?
- What did you learn that you didn't know before?
- What invitation does Jesus give us?
- How can a person answer yes to that invitation?
- What gift does God offer us?
- How can a person receive that gift?
- Why does God offer us a gift and an invitation?

Review the Scripture for today.

Pray, thanking God for the gift of eternal life and for his invitation to receive Jesus as Savior and Lord.

NOTE: This lesson will certainly cause many students who have not yet accepted Jesus as their Savior to think seriously about that decision. It is strongly recommended that you send a copy of the note from page 84 to parents, asking them to be watching for this interest from their children in the coming week.

Additional Bible Background

ADDITIONAL BIBLE BACKGROUND

During the discussion about accepting Jesus' invitation to be saved, the issue of baptism will probably arise. You can explain to students that

- Baptism allows us to live a new, clean, sinless life. Our sins are washed away! (See 1 Corinthians 6:11; Acts 22:16.)

- Baptism shows that we accept Jesus' death and burial (going into the water) and his resurrection (coming up out of the water). See Romans 6:1-4; Colossians 2:12.

- Baptism is a way of showing others and ourselves that we are committing our lives to follow Jesus and be like him (See Acts 2:38; Galatians 3:26, 27; 1 Peter 3:21.)

Dear Parent,

As you know, we are in the midst of a series of lessons concerning salvation. It is our goal to help each student understand what salvation is, how it is accomplished, and why we need it.

Today we talked about the choice that each of us has to accept Jesus' invitation to be saved. We are sure that many children who have not yet made a decision for Christ will be thinking about that choice this week.

We would ask you to be sensitive to that possibility. If your child has not yet accepted Christ as Savior, you may wish to talk to him or her about that decision this week.

As always, we are available to answer questions. You may also wish to contact the church office with questions and requests for assistance.

Teacher _____   Phone _____

Minister _____   Phone _____

Growing Up in Salvation

Scripture

"We should make ourselves pure—free from anything that makes body or soul unclean. We should try to become perfect in the way we live, because we respect God."   2 Corinthians 7:1, ICB

Goal

Learn that even though we are saved, we sometimes sin; yet we can still be right with God as long as we continue to put him first in our lives.

INTRODUCTION

On a piece of poster board, write:

1. Favorite food
2. Favorite color
3. Favorite TV show or movie
4. Favorite place to go
5. Favorite school subject

As the students arrive, give each student a large piece of manila paper and a marker or crayon. Ask the student to turn the piece of paper so that the long sides are to the left and right and the short sides are top and bottom. Then the student should write her favorites on the paper according to the categories listed on the poster board.

When the student has finished the list, use masking tape to attach the paper to the student's shoulders so that the list hangs in front of him. The students can then walk around and read each other's favorites.

DISCOVERY RALLY

Gather the students together in a large group.

WHAT'S THE GOOD WORD?

Choose a student to read the Scripture for today.

THE CHALLENGE

Bring a "magic slate." (These are in the coloring book sections of discount stores. The slate is a small board topped with a black wax base. This is overlaid with two plastic flaps, one thick and one thin. A plastic stick, mounted to the board, is used to draw on the plastic flap, which darkens because of the black wax underneath. When the plastic flap is lifted, the marks disappear.)

Show the students the unmarked slate. Then make a mark on the slate. Tell the students: **That mark represents a sin. What are some sins that students your age commit?** Each time they mention a sin, make a mark. **How can we be forgiven of our sins?** As they tell about Jesus' death, lift the plastic flap and show the clean slate. **What happens after people are saved? Does that mean they never ever sin again? We all still sin, even though we try not to. I may lie.** Make a mark. **But if I'm continuing to follow Jesus, I live in his forgiveness.** Lift the flap to erase the mark. **I may speak rudely.** Make a mark. **But if I'm continuing to follow Jesus, I live in his forgiveness.** Lift the flap to erase the mark. Ask a student to read 1 John 1:9.

Does this mean that I can sin all I want? No. I am supposed to reflect God's goodness, kindness, and love to others. When I sin, that's not what people see. Tell students that in their Discovery Centers today, they will learn more about living and growing in God's kingdom.

PRAYER

DISCOVERY CENTERS

1. FIGHTING TEMPTATION

plain white paper, markers or crayons, copy of the Temptation and Scriptures to Fight Them handout (page 90)

DO: Give each student a piece of paper. Have markers or crayons available. Ask each student to draw a sword on the piece of paper and design the hilt of the sword.

DISCUSS: What is temptation? (Temptation occurs when something wrong comes into our minds, and we want to do whatever that wrong thing is.) **Is temptation sin?** (No. Temptation is the thought of doing the wrong thing. Sin is doing it.) **Some sins happen in our minds, though. That can make it hard to know when it's temptation or sin. For example, hating someone is a sin that is in our thoughts. But the temptation to hate someone is in our thoughts, too. The temptation becomes a sin when we keep it in our thoughts and let it sink into our minds and feelings, and we let it stay there.**

DO: Read the list of temptations from the handout (page 90) until each student has chosen one thing that tempts him. The student writes that temptation at one of the corners of his paper. Then read to the student the Scripture reference that corresponds to the temptation. The student writes that Scripture reference on the sword he has drawn. If you have time, let the students look up their Scripture references and write the verse on the sword.

DISCUSS: Ask a student to read Matthew 4:1-11. Ask: **What did Jesus do when he was tempted? He quoted Scripture.** Ask another student to read Ephesians 6:17. **What is the Word of God called in this Scripture?** (Sword of the Spirit.) **When you are using God's Word to fight temptation, you might say you are "sword fighting." Learning to fight temptation is part of growing up in God's kingdom. What else helps us grow in God's kingdom?**

SALVATION The foundation for living with God | 87

2. THE BIG SHIRT RELAY

MATERIALS
a man's button-front shirt

DO: Choose one student to be the dresser. The other students form a line. Let the first student put the shirt on. Leave it unbuttoned. This student faces the student behind him and they hold hands. When you say "Go," the dresser takes off the shirt of the first student and puts it on the second student, while the two students are holding hands. (This will require that the shirt be turned inside out as it is lifted over the head of the students.) When the second student is wearing the shirt, she turns to face the next student in line. They hold hands, and the first student becomes the dresser while the original dresser goes to the end of the line. Continue this way until the shirt has been worn by all the students, including the original dresser. To make the game more exciting, you can time the students and do the game a second time or more to see if they can do it faster the next time(s).

DISCUSS: **Do your parents ever buy clothes that are a bit too large for you so you can grow into them?** Ask a student to read 1 Peter 2:2. **What is salvation? How do you think you can grow up in salvation?** Suggest Bible study, prayer, Scripture memory, thinking and wondering about God, practicing love and kindness.

Just as a new baby needs pure milk to nourish its body and help it grow, so a new Christian needs spiritual "food" to nourish his spirit and help him grow. Bible study, prayer, worship, and getting together with other Christians to learn about God are ways new believers can get this spiritual "milk."

3. REFLECTIONS

MATERIALS
none needed

DO: Divide the students into pairs. Ask each student to stand face to face with her partner. Choose one of the partners to be student A and one to be student B. Tell the students that A is a mirror, and B is to pretend to look into the mirror. Ask student B to make slow movements. Student A, being the mirror, must copy student B as exactly as possible, just like a reflection would. After a few minutes, let the partners trade jobs. B will be the mirror and A will make the slow movements.

DISCUSS: Ask a student to read 2 Corinthians 3:18. **What are we supposed to reflect?** (God's glory.) **What is God's glory?** (It is the revealing of who God is: his love, wisdom, and power.) **How can we reflect his love, wisdom, and power?** (First of all we trust him to lead us and give us what we need. When others see how God takes care of us, they see his love, wisdom, and power. Second, we do what Jesus said in Matthew 5:16.)

Ask a student to read Matthew 5:16. **What does Jesus want people to see in us? Why?** One way we grow and change to be more like Jesus every day is by choosing to act the way Jesus acted, speak the way Jesus spoke, and love the way Jesus loved.

DISCOVERERS' DEBRIEFING

If you have time to review, gather as a large group and discuss your young discoverers' findings. Ask the following questions:

- What is the most interesting thing you discovered today?
- What did you learn today that you didn't know before?
- Do people who are saved ever sin? Does this mean that they are not saved anymore?
- What should we do if we are saved, but we realize we have sinned?
- How can we grow and mature in God's kingdom?
- How can we reflect God and bring him glory?

Review the Scripture for today.

Pray, asking God to grow us up in his kingdom.

Temptations and Scriptures to Fight Them

Are you tempted to	Then quote this "sword":
Lose self-control?	1 Peter 1:13
Not listen when you should?	James 1:19
Feel hopeless?	Romans 15:13
Be prideful?	1 Corinthians 15:10
Not be thankful?	1 Thessalonians 5:18
Complain?	Philippians 2:14
Not pray?	1 Thessalonians 5:17
Be impatient?	Ephesians 4:2b
Disobey?	Hebrews 13:17
Be stingy or greedy?	2 Corinthians 9:7
Be rude?	Philippians 2:4
Be selfish?	Philippians 2:3
Discourage others?	Hebrews 10:24
Be disrespectful?	Matthew 7:12
Be afraid?	Psalm 56:11
Not forgive someone?	Colossians 3:13
Lie?	Colossians 3:9
Not keep a promise?	Ecclesiastes 5:5

How to Share the Good News

scripture

"Go into all the world and preach the good news to all creation. Whoever believes and is baptized will be saved."

Mark 16:15, 16

Goal

Learn simple and interesting ways to tell others the salvation message.

INTRODUCTION

As students arrive, give each student a copy of the What's the Good News? handout (page 96). Have crayons or markers available. Ask students to color only the spaces that have solid dots in them.

DISCOVERY RALLY

Gather students together in a large group.

WHAT'S THE GOOD WORD?

Choose a student to read the Scripture for today.

THE CHALLENGE

Ask the students what message they discovered when they colored the handout (page 96). Answer: Jesus is Lord. **That's what the good news is. Some people call it the gospel. Gospel means good news. The good news is that Jesus is Lord. He is the king. What is his kingdom? It is the kingdom of light. Is there any king more powerful than Jesus? No. Is there any king more loving and kind? No. Is there anything or anyone more important than our King Jesus? No.** Tell the students that today in their Discovery Centers they will learn how to tell the good news to other people.

PRAYER

DISCOVERY CENTERS

1. FOR THE WHOLE WORLD

DISCUSS: Ask a student to read God's promise to Abram in Genesis 12:1-3. Abram was the first person of the nation that would become Israel. God chose Abram and the nation of Israel. Read Genesis 12:3 again. Ask: **How many people did God want to bless?** Now ask a student to read Luke 2:8-11. **How many people was this good news for?** Ask another student to read Matthew 24:14. **To how many nations does God want to tell the good news?** Ask a student to read Revelation 5:9. **How many people did Jesus die for? God wants everyone to be in his kingdom.** Tell the students that they have already learned some ways to tell others about what Jesus has done for us: The Story in Your Hand and The String Story.

> **MATERIALS**
> 56-inch length of string or yarn for each student

DO: Review The Story in Your Hand that tells the story of salvation. (See page 57.) Give each student a string as suggested in Session 8 and review The String Story (pages 64, 65).

2. THE MESSAGE IN COLOR

MATERIALS
yellow, dark blue or gray, red, white, and green construction paper; yarn cut in 24-inch lengths; paper punch; scissors

DO: Give each student one piece of each of the five colors of construction paper. Ask the students to use a paper punch to punch two holes on the left side of one of the pages as if it were going to be placed in a notebook. Once one of the pages has holes, the student can use it as a template to show where the holes should be punched on the other pages. Now each student should stack his pages together with the yellow on top, and continuing as listed above, with green on the bottom. Then let the students thread a 24-inch piece of yarn through the holes and tie it to secure the side of this booklet. Cut off any excess yarn.

DISCUSS: Teach the students how to use these colors to tell the salvation message. Ask everyone to show the *yellow* page. Say: **This color will remind us of God: his shining power and his glorious heaven. God is perfect. He is good and kind. He never does anything wrong. Nothing bad or wrong or impure can live with him.**

Then ask everyone to show the *dark blue or gray* page. **This page reminds us of ourselves, because we do wrong things. We make wrong choices. We sin. Ask the person you are talking to what kinds of sins people commit. All people sin.**

Then ask everyone to show the *red* page. **This reminds us of Jesus' blood, because Jesus came to take the blame for our sins. He took our sins in himself, and he died on the cross, punished for our sins. Now that Jesus has been punished for our sins, God forgives us.**

Then ask everyone to show the *white* page. **We can be forgiven! We can be pure and perfect, without sin. We can live forever with God now! All we have to do is receive this free gift from God. Jesus wants to be our Lord and Savior!**

Then ask everyone to show the *green* page. **When we are saved, we need to keep** following Jesus and growing to be more like him every day. We read our Bibles, we pray, we meet with other believers and worship God.

If you have time, let the students practice this on each other.

(Note: This technique for sharing the good news is very old and is commonly called "The Wordless Book." Charles Spurgeon first used it in 1866, but he only had three colors. Another color was added later. The Wordless Book went on to be used by D.L. Moody, Fanny Crosby, and Amy Carmichael. During the first half of the 1900's the book began to be used by the Student Evangelism Fellowship. They added the green page. Black is typically the second color used, but out of racial respect, we avoid equating black with sin and prefer to use a navy blue or gray.)

3. THE GOOD NEWS BRACELET

MATERIALS
yarn, leather strip, or narrow ribbon cut into 8-inch lengths; yellow, dark blue or gray, red, white, and green beads

DO: Give each student a piece of yarn, leather, or ribbon. Also give each student one bead in each of the five colors listed above. Ask the students to thread these beads onto their yarn or ribbon in the order listed to make bracelets. Help them tie these loosely around their wrists. Then help them learn how to tell the salvation message with these colored beads in the same way described in Discovery Center #2.

DISCUSS: Why does God want us to tell this message to other people? Ask a student to read John 6:44. Can you think of someone right now who needs to hear the message about being saved? According to John 6:44, who must draw them to Jesus? Let's pray right now for these people and ask God to draw them to Jesus.

Discoverers' Debriefing
Debriefing

DISCOVERERS' DEBRIEFING

If you have time to review, gather as a large group and discuss your young discoverers' findings. Ask the following questions:

- **What is the most interesting thing you discovered today?**
- **What did you learn today that you didn't know before?**
- **What is the Good News?**
- **Why does God want us to tell the good news to every nation?**

Review telling the good news with colors, with strings, and with hand motions.

Review the Scripture for today.

Pray, thanking God for letting us be part of his plan to tell the world the good news. Thank God for letting us tell how everyone can become part of his kingdom of light.

What's the Good News?